This Journal Belongs To:

The Pink Self-Care Journal

One Year Of Guided Questions

For Women

21 EXERCISES

Follow us on Instagram

For promotions, giveaways and newest arrivals

Instagram: 21exercises_journals

Copyright © 2020 - 21 Exercises

Published by: The Alexander Publishing House

ISBN: 9798576492923

All rights reserved.

Disclaimer

This book is not intended to be a substitute for medical advice or treatment. Any person with a condition requiring medical attention should consult a qualified medical practitioner or suitable therapist.

The information provided in this book is stated to be truthful and consistent, in that any liability, in terms of inattention or otherwise, by any usage or abuse of any policies, processes, or directions contained within is the solitary and utter responsibility of the recipient reader. Under no circumstances will any legal responsibility or blame be held against the publisher for any reparation, damages, or monetary loss due to the information herein, either directly or indirectly.

Thank You

Dear Reader,

Thanks for purchasing our book.
We feel grateful to serve you with our carefully created:

The Pink Self-Care Journal

& Hope you enjoy, learn and find what you're looking for.

All the best,

21 Exercises

As a little thank you note,
we've three Free Personal-Growth exercises waiting for you.

Simply send an email to to exercises21@yahoo.com
Title the email "Pink Journal"

And we will send you Three Personal Growth Exercises for Free.

Introduction

Journaling isn't a task of boring, self-indulgent reflection. It's the art, the adventure of self-discovery. Find out your inner secrets, best ideas, thought patterns and dreams. Because awareness is the absolute key to living a better life. In this way your journaling habit becomes a valuable part of living a fine, prosperous and joyful life. This book covers questions for all important areas of life. From your love- or single life, money & prosperity to increasing your self-esteem and bringing awareness to your doubts and insecurities. Furthermore, there are multiple exercises in this book to help you develop your creativity. It's a complete guide for personal growth that helps you in living a life that feels satisfying & truthful to you. And we wish you nothing less.

•

How To Use This Journal

This journal is created for habitual use. Five questions per week, one-year long. Every week starts with a powerful quote and one repetitive question. To help you release your negative thoughts, worries and doubts. The rest of the week consists of four new, inspiring guided questions. Although this book is created to help you start the habit of journaling, it's not a prerequisite for the best experience. For you it might work best to go through the journal whenever you feel like it. Or instead of doing one question, doing a couple of questions per day. Since this is a how-to, however, these are our recommendations for using this journal:

1. Make it a daily habit, for example during your morning or evening routine.
2. Do multiple bing-journaling sessions: Go through 10 - 30 questions within a couple of days (a weekend for example). Buy snacks and smoothies. Schedule some time off and go on a binge-journaling journey.
3. Use the journal when you feel like using it. Don't give yourself rules, if you do one question it's okay, but if you feel like doing more, that's okay too. No schedules, no habit, no rules.

Week 1

Date: _____

"You're something between a dream and a miracle."

Elizabeth Barrett Browning

Breathe in. Breathe out.
Release all your negative thoughts, worries, and insecurities on paper.

Date: _____

Write down a big, seemingly unsolvable worry you currently have. And then, write down three different ways to look at it.

Date: _____

Write down a long list of things you would like to experience this year.

Date: _____

Create a drawing, or write a short story/poem/contemplation representing the story you need to tell this world.

Date: _____

What has life been trying to tell you over the past few months?

Week 2

Date: _____

"Remember that very little is needed to make a happy life."

Marcus Aurelius

Breathe in. Breathe out.
Release all your negative thoughts, worries, and insecurities on paper.

Date: _____

What three pieces of advice would you give to someone else in the exact same life situation as yourself?

Date: _____

Describe your perfect day of relaxation.

Date: _____

Make a chronological timeline with the most significant incidents that define who you are today.

Date: _____

What in your life currently does not feel authentic to you?

Week 3

Date: _____

"Not knowing when the dawn will come I open every door."

Emily Dickinson

Breathe in. Breathe out.
Release all your negative thoughts, worries, and insecurities on paper.

Date: _____

Write down all the reasons why you love yourself. Come up with at least seven reasons.

Date: _____

Write down an experience where you were about to give up, but continued anyway.

Date: _____

What are the top three things you would like to understand about yourself, and why?

Date: _____

Create a drawing, or write a story/poem/contemplation about being a woman in this world.

Week 4

Date: _____

"Nobody has ever measured, not even poets, how much the heart can hold."

Zelda Fitzgerald

Breathe in. Breathe out.
Release all your negative thoughts, worries, and insecurities on paper.

Date: _____

What do you consider feminine qualities?

Date: _____

What feminine qualities do you possess? What is the benefit of that?

Date: _____

Your definition of a good and healthy sex life.

Date: _____

Look at your answer from yesterday. How could you make this possible?

Week 5

Date: _____

"Better by far you should forget and smile than that you should remember and be sad."

Christina Rossetti

Breathe in. Breathe out.
Release all your negative thoughts, worries, and insecurities on paper.

Date: _____

What would the 7-year old version of you, think about you today?

Date: _____

What are your most important values?

Date: _____

Describe your perfect financial situation.

Date: _____

Create a drawing, or write a short story/contemplation/poem about a risk you should actually take.

Week 6

Date: _____

"What difference is there in the color of the soul?"

Solomon Northup

Breathe in. Breathe out.
Release all your negative thoughts, worries, and insecurities on paper.

Date: _____

Create a chronological list with the moments that made who you are today when it comes to love and relationships.

Date: _____

Describe your perfect physical situation.

Date: _____

What do you find most difficult about interacting with people? How can you deal better with this? Write down one or two ideas.

Date: _____

Describe the characteristics that are typical for your five closest friends.

Week 7

Date: _____

"To reach something good, it is useful to have gone astray."

St. Teresa of Avila

Breathe in. Breathe out.
Release all your negative thoughts, worries, and insecurities on paper.

Date: _____

Create a drawing, short story or poem to express your repressed anger.

Date: _____

Write down one or two memories about times where life surprised you in a truly fascinating way.

Date: _____

The best weekly diet that would work for you and makes you happy.

Date: _____

How does the way your parents loved each other affect your love life nowadays?

Week 8

Date: _____

"The future belongs to those who believe in the beauty of their dreams."

Eleanor Roosevelt

Breathe in. Breathe out.
Release all your negative thoughts, worries, and insecurities on paper.

Date: _____

Write down your bucket list. Which item could you actually do this year?

Date: _____

Pick an old photo of yourself that is at least four years old. Take a good look at the photo, and then reflect on it.

Date: _____

Create a drawing, or write a story/poem/contemplation about what gives you hope.

Date: _____

What makes you an attractive person to be around? Write down at least seven things.

Week 9

Date: _____

"If you look the right way, you can see that the whole world is a garden."

Frances Hodgson Burnett

Breathe in. Breathe out.
Release all your negative thoughts, worries, and insecurities on paper.

_____
_____
_____
_____
_____
_____
_____
_____
_____
_____
_____
_____
_____
_____

Date: _____

Twenty-five years from now, looking back on your life, what do you think will matter most to you?

Date: _____

When was the last time you truly surprised yourself?

Date: _******************_

If you had all the time in the world, what would you do first? Second? And third?

Date: _____

Create a drawing or write a short story/poem/contemplation about you at a party full of strangers.

Week 10

Date: _____

"To swallow and follow, whether old doctrine or new propaganda, is a weakness still dominating the human mind."

Charlotte Perkins Gilman

Breathe in. Breathe out.
Release all your negative thoughts, worries, and insecurities on paper.

Date: _____

Create a drawing, short story or poem that portrays your authentic self.

Date: _____

The mistakes you keep repeating when it comes to enjoying life.

Date: _____

When was the last time you felt the need to prove yourself to someone? How come?

Date: _____

What pattern are you repeating when it comes to your love life?

Week 11

Date: _____

"Love lights more fires than hate extinguishes."

Ella Wheeler Wilcox

Breathe in. Breathe out.
Release all your negative thoughts, worries, and insecurities on paper.

Date: _____

How you think the world sees you.

Date: _____

Write down a (an imaginative) letter to your partner or future partner, so that he or she could understand you better.

Date: _____

What beliefs and thoughts do you associate with being a woman?

Date: _____

- Create a drawing, short story or poem that portrays your image.

Week 12

Date: _____

"There is no exquisite beauty… without some strangeness in the proportion."

Edgar Allan Poe

Breathe in. Breathe out.
Release all your negative thoughts, worries, and insecurities on paper.

Date: _____

Write down all the things you worry about, that are outside of your control.

Date: _____

Create a chronological timeline with the most significant moments where fear stopped you from doing what you had to do.

Date: _____

Look in the mirror for at least one minute straight. Describe what you see and feel.

Date: _____

How are you most frequently misunderstood by other people?

Week 13

Date: _____

"Happiness is like a butterfly which, when pursued, is always beyond our grasp, but, if you will sit down quietly, may alight upon you."

Nathaniel Hawthorne

Breathe in. Breathe out.
Release all your negative thoughts, worries, and insecurities on paper.

Date: _____

Create a timeline representing your life over the last 12 months.

Date: _____

Your definition of freedom.

Date: _____

What makes you feel grateful for your love life/ dating life of the past?
Write down at least seven things.

Date: _____

Write down five small things you can do on a regular basis to improve your relationship with yourself.

Week 14

Date: _____

"Kind words can be short and easy to speak, but their echoes are truly endless."

Mother Teresa

Breathe in. Breathe out.
Release all your negative thoughts, worries, and insecurities on paper.

_____
_____
_____
_____
_____
_____
_____
_____
_____
_____
_____
_____
_____
_____
_____
_____

Date: _____

How has advertising affected your view of being a woman in a negative way?

Date: _____

What rules are standing in the way of your happiness right now?

Date: _******************_

What kind of persons make you curious?

Date: _____

Create a timeline of how you would like your life to turn out to be over the next year.

Week 15

Date: _____

"For there is a bigger you awaiting and the problems of today will soon be seen as small and insignificant tomorrow."

C.W. V. Straaten

Breathe in. Breathe out.
Release all your negative thoughts, worries, and insecurities on paper.

Date: _____

What are the five people in your life, you are seeking approval from the most.

Date: _____

Create a drawing or write a short story/poem about your insecurities.

Date: _____

How could you bring more harmony to your life?

Date: _____

Describe your ideal three weeks of traveling.

Week 16

Date: _____

"The power of finding beauty in the humblest things makes home happy and life lovely."

Louisa May Alcott

Breathe in. Breathe out.
Release all your negative thoughts, worries, and insecurities on paper.

_____
_____
_____
_____
_____
_____
_____
_____
_____
_____
_____
_____
_____
_____
_____

Date: _____

How would you describe yourself?

Date: _____

How would the people closest to you describe you?

Date: _____

How was your first experience with falling in love?

Date: _____

What experiences or people are often triggering your negative self-dialogue?

_____
_____
_____
_____
_____
_____
_____
_____
_____
_____
_____
_____
_____
_____
_____
_____
_____
_____
_____
_____
_____
_____
_____

Week 17

Date: _____

"As she realized what might have been, she grew to be thankful for what was."

Elizabeth Gaskell

Breathe in. Breathe out.
Release all your negative thoughts, worries, and insecurities on paper.

_____
_____
_____
_____
_____
_____
_____
_____
_____
_____
_____
_____
_____
_____
_____
_____

Date: _____

What beliefs you once had about yourself are now gone?

Date: _____

Create a drawing, short story or poem to express your sexual energy.

Date: _____

Authentic self-expression is an attraction magnet. How can authentic self-expression help you to attract the right persons into your life?

Date: _____

What is the role of mass media in shaping our beliefs for this world? Is it a message of love or one of fear they share? Reflect on that answer.

Week 18

Date: _____

"How wonderful it is that nobody need wait a single moment before starting to improve the world."

Anne Frank

Breathe in. Breathe out.
Release all your negative thoughts, worries, and insecurities on paper.

_____
_____
_____
_____
_____
_____
_____
_____
_____
_____
_____
_____
_____
_____
_____
_____

Date: _____

Create a timeline representing your appearance over the last 10 years.

(Tip: use old photos:)

Date: _____

What fears you once had, are now gone?

Date: _____

What courageous choice you made as a teenager is still benefiting you today?

Date: _____

What conversations you had this year gave you new insights about life/yourself?

Week 19

Date: _____

"Challenges are gifts that force us to search for a new center of gravity. Don't fight them. Just find a new way to stand."

Oprah Winfrey

Breathe in. Breathe out.
Release all your negative thoughts, worries, and insecurities on paper.

Date: _____

What problems in your life could actually be opportunities?

Date: _____

What do you consider masculine qualities?

Date: _____

What masculine qualities do you possess? What is the benefit of that?

Date: _____

Write down three things you can do this month to give yourself a better feeling, without feeling guilty.

Week 20

Date: _____

"It is never too late to be what you might have been."

George Eliot

Breathe in. Breathe out.
Release all your negative thoughts, worries, and insecurities on paper.

Date: _____

Write down a list of maximum seven thoughts that you frequently have that only bring you stress and unhappiness.

Date: _____

Look at your answers from the previous page. Now rephrase these thoughts in an empowering way.

Date: _____

Write down three memories where life/God/a Higher Power really helped you in a surprising way.

Date: _____

Create a conversation: Meeting the version of you of one year ago in a bar, after hours, in your hometown.

Week 21

Date: _____

"Imagination does not become great until human beings, given the courage and the strength, use it to create."

Maria Montessori

Breathe in. Breathe out.
Release all your negative thoughts, worries, and insecurities on paper.

_____
_____
_____
_____
_____
_____
_____
_____
_____
_____
_____
_____
_____
_____
_____

Date: _____

What did you once believed about love, but not anymore?

Date: _____

What social conditions just don't work for you?

Date: _____

Statements you want to live by.

Date: _____

Where in your life could you use more integrity? How can you make this happen?

Week 22

Date: _____

"Everyone on Earth, they'd tell us, was carrying around an unseen history, and that alone deserved some tolerance."

Michelle Obama

Breathe in. Breathe out.
Release all your negative thoughts, worries, and insecurities on paper.

_____
_____
_____
_____
_____
_____
_____
_____
_____
_____
_____
_____
_____
_____

Date: _____

Create a drawing or write a short story/poem/contemplation about your teenage years.

Date: _____

How do social media and advertising influence your self-image?

Date: _____

Write down four reasons why you love humanity.

Date: _____

What does your ideal morning look like?

Week 23

Date: _____

"I am convinced that there are times in everybody's experience when there is so much to be done, that the only way to do it is to sit down and do nothing."

Fanny Fern

Breathe in. Breathe out.
Release all your negative thoughts, worries, and insecurities on paper.

Date: _____

When was the last time you felt truly alive?

Date: _____

What things can you realistically do this month to improve your health?

Date: _____

Describe your comfort zone: The things, people, habits, etc., you need to feel safe.

Date: _____

What beliefs you once had about women are now gone?

Week 24

Date: _____

"If we take care of the moments, the years will take care of themselves."

Maria Edgeworth

Breathe in. Breathe out.
Release all your negative thoughts, worries, and insecurities on paper.

_____
_____
_____
_____
_____
_____
_____
_____
_____
_____
_____
_____
_____
_____
_____

Date: _____

What makes you physically attractive? Write down at least seven things.

Date: _____

How would you describe a healthy romantic relationship?

Date: _____

How would you describe the road towards self-acceptance.

Date: _____

When was the last you told a lie to protect your own image?

Week 25

Date: _____

"A very small degree of hope is sufficient to cause the birth of love."

Stendhal

Breathe in. Breathe out.
Release all your negative thoughts, worries, and insecurities on paper.

_____
_____
_____
_____
_____
_____
_____
_____
_____
_____
_____
_____
_____
_____
_____
_____

Date: _____

Make a whole list of joyful, and mindful things you could do the next time you feel bored, lonely or down.

Date: _____

Create a drawing, or write a short story/poem/contemplation portraying you as your most confident, courageous, kind and sexy self.

Date: _____

Write down one or two memories from recent years that makes you feel exhilarated.

Date: _____

Write down ten things that always make you smile.

Week 26

Date: _____

"Be glad. Be good. Be brave."

Eleanor Hodgman Porter

Breathe in. Breathe out.
Release all your negative thoughts, worries, and insecurities on paper.

Date: _____

When was the last time you were too hard on yourself? Why did you choose that reaction?

Date: _____

Create a drawing, or write a contemplation, short story or poem expressing your critical self.

Date: _____

Write down at least twelve of your possessions you could live easily without.

Date: _____

Who and what makes you feel optimistic about yourself and about life in general?

Week 27

Date: _____

"If we had no winter, the spring would not be so pleasant: if we did not sometimes taste of adversity, prosperity would not be so welcome."

Anne Bradstreet

Breathe in. Breathe out.
Release all your negative thoughts, worries, and insecurities on paper.

_____
_____
_____
_____
_____
_____
_____
_____
_____
_____
_____
_____
_____
_____
_____
_____

Date: _____

Create a chronological timeline describing your working life.

Date: _____

What happens with the thoughts, the feelings that you don't express?
Where are they going?

Date: _____

What about your health makes you feel grateful?

Date: _____

Describe your pattern of procrastination.

Week 28

Date: _____

"I am not afraid of storms, for I am learning how to sail my ship."

Louisa May Alcott

Breathe in. Breathe out.
Release all your negative thoughts, worries, and insecurities on paper.

Date: _____

When was the last time your mind stopped your enthusiasm?
How did you feel about that?

Date: _____

What words of advice would your 80-year-old self give to you now?

Date: _____

What is the main reason you feel the determination to go on this journey of self-discovery?

Date: _____

Create a drawing, or write a contemplation/short story/poem representing your relationship with your parents.

Week 29

Date: _____

"There's a place in the soul where you've never been wounded."

Meister Eckhart

Breathe in. Breathe out.
Release all your negative thoughts, worries, and insecurities on paper.

Date: _____

What small habits or tiny deeds are having a major influence on your overall well-being?

Date: _____

Which people on the planet inspire you and why?

Date: _____

What conventional thoughts about women do work for you?

Date: _____

Write down a list of things you would like to happen in your life.

Week 30

Date: _____

"It'll be just lovely for you to play -- it'll be so hard. And there's so much more fun when it is hard!"

Eleanor Hodgman Porter

Breathe in. Breathe out.
Release all your negative thoughts, worries, and insecurities on paper.

_____
_____
_____
_____
_____
_____
_____
_____
_____
_____
_____
_____
_____
_____
_____

Date: _____

Make a drawing, or write a story/poem/contemplation about a past achievement that makes you feel proud.

Date: _____

What conventional thoughts about women, just don't work for you?

Date: _____

Write down at least seven positive and encouraging statements/affirmations you deserve.

Date: _____

The last time you spoke up for something greater than yourself.

Week 31

Date: _____

"Those who have not found the heaven below, will fail of it above."

Emily Dickinson

Breathe in. Breathe out.
Release all your negative thoughts, worries, and insecurities on paper.

Date: _____

A list of all the people in your life you feel grateful for.

Date: _____

Write down your favorite wardrobe.

Date: _____

Create a drawing, short story or poem to express joy for life.

Date: _____

What do you find most difficult about the female body? How can you use this to your benefit?

Week 32

Date: _____

"Come friends, it's not too late to seek a newer world."

Alfred Lord Tennyson

Breathe in. Breathe out.
Release all your negative thoughts, worries, and insecurities on paper.

Date: _____

Create a drawing or write a short story/poem/contemplation/contemplation about your early childhood.

Date: _____

The one mistake you keep repeating when it comes to your financial situation.

Date: _____

What does your sex life say about you as a person?

Date: _____

Why you're grateful for your closest friends.

Week 33

Date: _____

"Ah, it is impossible." "No, it is only very difficult - so very difficult that I shall be sure to accomplish it!"

E.D.E.N. Southworth

Breathe in. Breathe out.
Release all your negative thoughts, worries, and insecurities on paper.

Date: _____

Write down a list of seven thoughts that always makes you feel better.

Date: _____

Describe your perfect career/professional life.

Date: _____

How do you most often deal with confrontation? What are two or three better ways to deal with it?

Date: _____

What makes you jealous of other women? Try to be honest and list down all the reasons.

Week 34

Date: _____

"There are no little things. Little things are the hinges of the universe."

Fanny Fern

Breathe in. Breathe out.
Release all your negative thoughts, worries, and insecurities on paper.

_____
_____
_____
_____
_____
_____
_____
_____
_____
_____
_____
_____
_____
_____

Date: _____

What are you most trying to control in life? Write down two or three things.

Date: _____

Describe your perfect date night.

Date: _____

What are your biggest fears when it comes to your love life?

Date: _____

Create a drawing, short story or poem to express your courage.

Week 35

Date: _____

"Ah! There is nothing like staying at home, for real comfort."

Jane Austen

Breathe in. Breathe out.
Release all your negative thoughts, worries, and insecurities on paper.

Date: _____

What could other people learn from you?

Date: _____

Write down three things you could do to help yourself in difficult times.

Date: _____

What two or three things can you do this month to improve your personal relationships?

Date: _____

What did you learn about attachment in the last few months?

Week 36

Date: _____

"We do not need magic to transform our world. We carry all the power we need inside ourselves already."

J.K. Rowling

Breathe in. Breathe out.
Release all your negative thoughts, worries, and insecurities on paper.

_____
_____
_____
_____
_____
_____
_____
_____
_____
_____
_____
_____
_____
_____
_____

Date: _____

Create a drawing, or write a contemplation/poem/short story about living life to the fullest.

Date: _____

Write down one or two memories from your teenage years that make you feel grateful.

Date: _____

What kind of recklessness do you secretly like and why?

Date: _____

Write down five things you could do to integrate more calm/zen/mindfulness into your daily life.

Week 37

Date: _____

"Nothing contributes so much to tranquilize the mind as a steady purpose."

Mary Shelley

Breathe in. Breathe out.
Release all your negative thoughts, worries, and insecurities on paper.

Date: _____

Create a drawing, or write a short story/poem/contemplation to express your love to the world.

Date: _____

How do you try to seek security in life?

Date: _____

What does it take to gain your trust?

Date: _____

How could you take utmost care of your most precious qualities?

Week 38

Date: _____

"Life has much of harmony yet in store for you."

Fanny Fern

Breathe in. Breathe out.
Release all your negative thoughts, worries, and insecurities on paper.

Date: _____

Create a drawing, or write a short story/poem/contemplation expressing your unique female qualities.

Date: _____

What would you like to receive when it comes to relationships?

Date: _____

How could you loosen up a bit more?

Date: _____

What qualities/characteristics do you admire in other people?

Week 39

Date: _____

"But the future must be met, however stern and iron it be."

Elizabeth Gaskell

Breathe in. Breathe out.
Release all your negative thoughts, worries, and insecurities on paper.

Date: _____

What patterns are you continuously repeating when it comes to your health?

_____
_____
_____
_____
_____
_____
_____
_____
_____
_____
_____
_____
_____
_____
_____
_____
_____
_____
_____
_____
_____
_____
_____
_____
_____

Date: _____

What beliefs about money you once had, are now gone?

Date: _____

What you would do with ten million dollars?

Date: _____

What three things could you do to make this month great?

Week 40

Date: _____

"We must not wish for the disappearance of our troubles but for the grace to transform them."

Simone Weil

Breathe in. Breathe out.
Release all your negative thoughts, worries, and insecurities on paper.

_____
_____
_____
_____
_____
_____
_____
_____
_____
_____
_____
_____

Date: _____

Create a drawing, or write a contemplation/poem/short story about your journey of self-discovery.

Date: _____

What simple pleasures did you enjoy this week?

Date: _____

What beauty did you see this year?

Date: _____

What are your thoughts on extraterrestrial life? And how is this opinion interfering with how you see life on earth?

Week 41

Date: _____

"Conventionality is not morality."

Charlotte Bronte

Breathe in. Breathe out.
Release all your negative thoughts, worries, and insecurities on paper.

Date: _____

Write down three things you can do to reduce the pressure on yourself.

Date: _____

Write down five things you look forward to in life.

Date: _____

What emotion(s) mostly run your life?

Date: _____

How can you better deal with the emotion(s) that are most present in your life?

Week 42

Date: _____

"I dwell in possibility…"

Emily Dickinson

Breathe in. Breathe out.
Release all your negative thoughts, worries, and insecurities on paper.

Date: _____

Love is the way. What would you love to do every day?

Date: _____

If you had only one more year to live, what would you love to create?

Date: _____

Write down three or more things you can do to improve the energy levels in your home.

Date: _____

Is your physical appearance a representation of who you really are? Why or why not?

Week 43

Date: _____

"This above all: to thine own self be true."

William Shakespeare

Breathe in. Breathe out.
Release all your negative thoughts, worries, and insecurities on paper.

Date: _ _ _ _ _ _ _ _ _ _ _ _ _ _ _ _ _

Create a drawing or write a short story/poem/contemplation about the beautiful (im)perfections of your body.

Date: _____

What does your ideal night routine look like?

Date: _____

What barriers have you built up against love?

Date: _____

Write down a list of things you would like to own.

Week 44

Date: _____

"But the cloud never comes in that quarter of the horizon from which we watch for it."

Elizabeth Gaskell

Breathe in. Breathe out.
Release all your negative thoughts, worries, and insecurities on paper.

_____
_____
_____
_____
_____
_____
_____
_____
_____
_____
_____
_____
_____
_____
_____

Date: _____

What lessons did you learn in the past few months?

Date: _____

A conversation with yourself as a teenager.

Date: _____

How can you be more truthful to others?

Date: _____

How can you be more truthful to yourself?

Week 45

Date: _____

"Where wisdom reigns, there is no conflict between thinking and feeling."

Carl Gustav Jung

Breathe in. Breathe out.
Release all your negative thoughts, worries, and insecurities on paper.

Date: _____

Create a drawing, or write a short story/poem/contemplation representing your feelings about being with children.

Date: _____

Two or three questions you would like to ask one of your role models.
And what they might answer.

Date: _____

Are you more a giver or a taker in personal relationships? Why?

Date: _____

What are you willing to sacrifice for becoming who you want to become?

Week 46

Date: _____

"That it will never come again is what makes life so sweet."

Emily Dickinson

Breathe in. Breathe out.
Release all your negative thoughts, worries, and insecurities on paper.

Date: _____

Why do you deserve love? Write down at least three reason.

Date: _____

Your three favorite sexual fantasies.

Date: _____

Describe your ideal workweek.

Date: _____

What are your three favorite books and why?

Week 47

Date: _____

"Never close your lips to those whom you have already opened your heart."

Charles Dickens

Breathe in. Breathe out.
Release all your negative thoughts, worries, and insecurities on paper.

Date: _____

What do you have to offer your (potential) partner in a relationship?

Date: _____

What five people are triggering you the most? Why?

Date: _____

How you most often sabotage your own happiness.

Date: _____

Create a drawing, or write a contemplation/poem/short story portraying your hopes for the future.

Week 48

Date: _____

"Nobody can hurt me without my permission."

Mahatma Gandhi

Breathe in. Breathe out.
Release all your negative thoughts, worries, and insecurities on paper.

Date: _____

Create a drawing, short story or poem about the last time you hit rock bottom. (Give it a touch of hope, honoring how you were able to pull yourself through! And/or use humor)

Date: _____

How would you define ambition?

Date: _____

Draw a graph representing your finances over the last 3 years.

Date: _____

Write down three things you like about your money situation right now. And write down three things you would like to have more of when it comes to money.

Week 49

Date: _____

"Perhaps it is better to wake up after all, even to suffer, rather than to remain a dupe to illusions all one's life."

Kate Chopin

Breathe in. Breathe out.
Release all your negative thoughts, worries, and insecurities on paper.

Date: _____

Three good deeds you could do this month.

Date: _____

How would you like people to remember you?

Date: _____

What was your favorite age growing up and why?

Date: _____

What about love scares you?

Week 50

Date: _____

"Authenticity is the key to attraction."

Zen Mirrors

Breathe in. Breathe out.
Release all your negative thoughts, worries, and insecurities on paper.

_____
_____
_____
_____
_____
_____
_____
_____
_____
_____
_____
_____
_____
_____

Date: _____

Create a drawing, or write a short story/contemplation/poem how you have grown as a person this year.

Date: _____

Write down ten songs that bring you always in a happy mood.

Date: _******_

Write down one or two childhood memories that make you feel wonderful.

Date: _____

How has Hollywood/the movie industry affected your view on love in a negative or unrealistic way?

Week 51

Date: _____

"Turn your wounds into wisdom."

Oprah Winfrey

Breathe in. Breathe out.
Release all your negative thoughts, worries, and insecurities on paper.

Date: _____

Create a drawing, or write a short story/contemplation/poem about how your flaws are an opportunity to grow.

Date: _____

Describe gratitude in your own words. And write down three things that made you feel grateful today.

_____
_____
_____
_____
_____
_____
_____
_____
_____
_____
_____
_____
_____
_____
_____
_____
_____
_____
_____
_____
_____
_____
_____
_____
_____

Date: _____

What do you find most difficult about your life right now? And write down three unconventional and optimistic ways to look at it.

Date: _____

Write down seven small things you can do this month to make an incredible improvement to your life.

Week 52

Date: _____

"Do your best, And leave the rest, 'Twill all come right Some day or night."

Anna Sewell

Breathe in. Breathe out.
Release all your negative thoughts, worries, and insecurities on paper.

_____
_____
_____
_____
_____
_____
_____
_____
_____
_____
_____
_____
_____
_____
_____
_____
_____

Date: _____

What wounds from the past are still running your life in a negative way? How can you go towards transcending these wounds?

Date: _____

If you were given a blank page upon which you can recreate your life, what would you create?

Date: _____

Write a letter to yourself to be opened six months from now.

Date: _____

Who would you like to be one year from now?

This Has Been:

The Pink
Self-Care Journal

Follow us on Instagram

For promotions, giveaways and newest arrivals
Instagram: 21exercises_journals

Manufactured by Amazon.ca
Bolton, ON